THE
NANOSECOND
SALESPERSON

CHUCK REAVES, CSP, CPAE, CSO

Chuck Reaves, CSP, CPAE, CSO

The Nanosecond Salesperson
© 2009 Chuck Reaves, CSP, CPAE
ISBN: 1450503462
ISBN-13: 9781450503464

SaleSSuiteS Holdings, LLC
5952 Allee Way
Braselton, GA 30517
770.965.5595

Printed in the United States of America

TABLE OF CONTENTS

Introduction   Page i

Chapter One: The Situation   Page 1

Chapter Two: The Proposal   Page 5

Chapter Three: The Call   Page 9

Chapter Four: The Encounter   Page 13

Chapter Five: Kaizen   Page 17

Chapter Six: The Meeting   Page 21

Chapter Seven: Questions   Page 27

Chapter Eight: Kaizen 2   Page 37

Chapter Nine: The Event   Page 43

Chapter Ten: The Event 2   Page 51

Chapter Eleven: Delegating   Page 59

Chapter Twelve: Game Over   Page 67

Epilogue   Page 79

INTRODUCTION

Got a minute?
No?
Me either.
Too busy.

The number one trend in sales is "fast". Customers want things to happen quickly. Many times the customer will settle for a slightly-inferior solution if it can be delivered sooner than the best solution.

00:00
The number one trend in sales is "fast". Customers are like us, they want everything fast.

We want things fast. So do our customers.

We live in a world of fast – and faster. We want fast food and we want it ready when we're ready and we want the transaction to happen fast.

We don't want to wait in line for anything anymore.

In the North American culture we will actually pace in front of a microwave oven! A minute for a cup of hot water is entirely too long.

If the line is too long at Starbucks, we will deny ourselves our coffee. As a result, Starbucks replaced their machines with faster ones and are looking for a technology and/or process that will accelerate the procedure even more. We want fast food – the ability to order, purchase and receive food in about the same time it takes a NASCAR racer to make a pit stop.

We want things fast and so do our customers.

Proof: you are driving down a multi-lane street. Up ahead there is an intersection with a traffic light and the light is red. Do you assess the cars currently sitting at the light? There's a school bus – no way we're going to get behind that one! The out-of-state minivan with luggage piled on top – no way.

We are talking seconds here, mere seconds. And yet we think our customer is going to have time for chit chat and doughnuts before we actually get into our call? Think again. Those days are over. Some salespeople realize it.

As sales professionals, we need to learn how to deliver everything we do faster than ever. Your next sales call needs to happen faster than the last one - but not as fast as the one after that. Acceleration of the sales process can be the difference between success and failure for most salespeople.

For example, vendors selling to Wal-Mart are given a subtle reminder. As they talk to the appropriate buyer, a thirty-minute timer is running right in front of them.

And while the speed is accelerating, the quality of the call needs to improve as well. Customers want quality information that will allow them to make quality decisions and they want it fast.

Oh yeah, the cost of sales (COS) must also decline. Since fewer customers seem to be able to make time for long dinners and golf games, that may take care of itself when travel and entertainment (T&E) are calculated. For your organization to be more profitable, your COS needs to go down.

So, spend less, sell better and do it faster. Is this the sales game you want to play? It is, in fact, the new sales game for the major leagues. If you want to play in the majors, learn the new rules.

Here are some concepts for you to consider. If you replace a face-to-face sales call with an electronic call, time is saved and your COS is lower. Can you do that effectively enough that the quality of the call is actually higher as well?

Make that happen and you're selling better, faster and at a lower COS.

Need to do a product demo? You and your customer will need to schedule time together. You will need to factor in travel time and travel cost. It may be days or even weeks before you can coordinate your schedules. This will be days or weeks during which time your customer is not financially benefiting from your offering. It will also be days or weeks where your company is not reaping the financial benefits of making the sale. It may also be a time when you are not making bonus for being over quota – or maybe even not making quota. It is also allowing time for your competitors to go after the same customer. Waiting is not an option.

Replace the face-to-face call with a video email. You will be making a customized, targeted sales presentation that addresses the same customer's senses as a face-to-face call except for smell. How often does your customer need to smell you or your products to make a buying decision? It's simple and relatively easy to do. Supplement the video email with some generic collateral materials and it can be a better, faster and lower cost sales presentation.

You can identify a prospect, conduct a qualified and quantified needs analysis, do a qualified and quantified feature-benefit-solution presentation, overcome their price resistance with a qualified and quantified cost justification and close the sale before your competitors can schedule an appointment.

Or, your competitors can do that to you.

It's your choice.

> 00:00
> Sales is a science,
> not an art

Sales is changing. The sales department is finally being given access to the benefits of the programs, processes, technology and even the tools that other departments have enjoyed.

It's our turn.

Sales is a science, not an art. As such, it is a measurable, predictable replicatable science. Yes, I know, every salesperson is different and every customer is different. In fact, every customer is different on every sales call. Their needs are changing, their industry is changing and their competitors are changing. We need to be able to respond quickly and profitably to the rapid changes that are happening in their businesses in order to respond quickly and rapidly to the changes that are happening in ours.

Therefore, sales is changing.

Why a nanosecond instead of a minute? We need to learn to think "faster", as in "how can I do this faster?" If we set a goal to accomplish something in an hour that has traditionally taken a week, and we achieve that goal, were we successful? Not if the same task could have been completed in ten minutes.

Setting extraordinary goals is the first step to achieving extraordinary success. Set your goals higher than the actual results that you want. That way, even if you fall short, you will still have made significant improvements.

The CEO of a software company called and said he had purchased another company with a nine month sales cycle. As it turns out, he could not afford to wait nine months for the sales to begin improving and he was looking for help. I asked him what he would like for the sales cycle to be. He had not really thought it through but he said that if a couple of months could be shaved off of the sales process he would be okay.

After hanging up the phone I sat and thought about what he had told me on the telephone and I began developing a plan and process for his situation. (In this book you will be exposed to these.) I also wrote down a time frame for his sales cycle, my target objective for him, which I will share with you in a minute.

Within a month, his top salesperson had closed a sale with a major firm in seven weeks.

During that time, we had streamlined the process, developed tools the salespeople could use, developed tools the clients and potential clients could use to expedite the sales process and we had shifted the thinking of the salespeople.

What was my objective for the sales cycle timeframe? Nine days. I missed my goal of reducing their time-to-market from nine months to nine days, but they were at least able to reduce it to seven weeks. Were they happy? You bet!

My current objective for them is nine minutes. Even if I fail, we will probably have reduced their sales cycle to nine days.

It is time to change the way you think about sales in order to capitalize on all of the other changes that are happening in the profession of selling.

So how is this change happening? Real Sales Automation (RSA) is helping. Kaizen for Sales is great foundation. Supply Chain Selling, selling to the customer's customer (selling <u>through</u>, not <u>to</u>) is another approach.

Is this too much too quickly? Don't have time to digest all of this? No problem.

Here is a quick read that will lay it all out for you in allegorical form. In about 100 pages you'll be up to speed.

"In the history of recorded time, no customer has ever said, 'Your price is too high,' and meant it."   - Chuckism #6

CHAPTER ONE: THE SITUATION

Ed turned on the lights as he entered the sales offices of International Virtual Communications (IVC). This was not uncommon. Since Ed joined the company eight years ago, he had often been the first person in the office in the mornings and, many times, the last to leave. The difference now was that Ed did not walk, talk or move as fast – a sign of his disappointment with his own performance.

IVC was a cutting-edge company in many ways. The technologists were developing new products and services almost daily. The industries where they sold and the customers they served acknowledged IVC as the most innovative company around. Ed had managed to keep up with the fast pace of change and felt like he understood the products and their applications as well as anyone.

What he could not understand was why his sales were falling.

Even though younger salespeople would ask him for advice on selling, on how specific products and their features worked, his own production was falling.

> **00:00**
> **Our minds, bodies and spirits respond to our perception of our level of success**

Ed made his way to the break room, turned on the coffee maker and walked to his cubicle. He could download his emails while the coffee maker warmed up. His cubicle was like a second home to him. There were pictures of his wife and several pictures of his children: his daughter's wedding picture, his son's college graduation picture – all reminders of past successes.

There was the picture of Ed and his wife, Katherine, at the national sales meeting at the Princess Hotel in Acapulco when Ed was honored as the top salesperson in the company. What an event that had been. After only three years with IVC, he had attained the enviable status of the highest producer. Now, five years later, he was seeing entire quarters go by without him making quota in a single month.

Ed wondered how long IVC would tolerate his lack of production. All salespeople fall into slumps from time to time and certainly this was nothing new for Ed. What was different now was that he seemed unable to pull himself out of the lull. He wondered if, maybe, his selling days were over.

> 00:00
> The CSO has the same responsibilities for sales as the CFO has for finance: vision, strategy, higher-level thinking

As the emails made their way into his inbox Ed heard the coffee maker's welcomed beep and knew his first cup of the day was ready.

Returning from the break room, Ed heard some other people stirring around in the office. Rather than socialize, he went back to his cubicle and scanned the messages on his screen.

The first one he always read was the Sales Summary Report. This was a daily listing of what his sales team and the other teams around the country had accomplished the previous day. Glancing over at the picture of him and Katherine in Acapulco, he remembered the day when opening this report was a boost to his ego. Now it was just another reminder of his lack of success.

> 00:00
> Loyalty between employees and employers is diminishing; both are beginning to see the other as replaceable

His office was doing well. For the past few months Ed's fellow salespeople were keeping the Atlanta sales office on top. It helped, of course, that the company was headquartered in the same building. Salespeople could regularly network with the movers and shakers in the company as well as the brilliant engineers who were always working on the next new thing.

The Regional Sales Managers (RSM's) in Atlanta were some of the best sales leaders. They had to be. They were in the fishbowl atmosphere of any sales organization co-located with the corporate offices. It was too easy for salespeople and sales managers to encounter executives in search of results. Accolades were not common and questions were frequent.

IVC's top sales leader was Mike Anderson. He held the unusual title of Chief Sales Officer. IVC was on the cutting edge of organizational structure as well. The idea of having a sales leader on par with the leaders of operations, finance and technology was not, originally, their idea. It came up at a board meeting when the president of the company, Andrea Mueller, had made a presentation explaining that the company was moving to become more customer focused. A marketing-focused or sales-focused organization would be better, she explained, for capturing more market share. IVC's products and services were the best in the market but no product will sell itself.

> **00:00**
> No product has ever sold itself. Ever. If you thinks yours will, take a customer out to your warehouse at 2 AM and listen

Some of the board disagreed by saying that the company had grown because of the superiority of the technology and the quality of manufacturing. But one Director, Malcolm Harris, challenged the traditional thinking. He had built several successful companies, some high tech and some that were very basic. He disagreed with the concept that great products will sell themselves.

> **00:00**
> The "Better Mousetrap" myth

"Thinking that if you build a better mousetrap the world will beat a path to your door," he had said, "denies three assumptions. One is that the world knows you have a better mousetrap – that's the function of marketing. Another is that the world knows where your door is – that's sales. Finally, the world has to know they have mice. If they don't have mice, or don't realize they have mice, they're not going to be interested in your mousetrap no matter how good it is."

Mr. Harris waited for his remarks to sink in and then stood up and said, "I agree that it is time for IVC to start focusing on what you can do for your customers, not just what you can do. And if you're serious about sales, why don't you have a Chief Sales Officer? You have a CFO watching the numbers and a COO keeping an eye on the day-to-day stuff. You even have a Chief Technology Officer to corral all those smart people in the tech center. If you're serious about sales, you'll prove it by putting a CSO in place." With that he sat down.

> **00:00**
> Customers don't want our products and services, nor do they want what they can do. They only want what our products and services can do for them right now

Whenever Mr. Harris sat down everyone understood he had nothing more to say on a subject. And when one of the largest shareholders and most influential Board members says something, it is usually best to take it to heart.

Before long, IVC had a CSO. Mike Anderson was chosen after the Board had checked off on the criteria for the job.

This was especially important to Ed this morning. Nestled in all of the other emails was one from "AndersonM". Ed's heart stopped beating for a moment when he saw it. When he moved his cursor to open the email, Ed noticed it was vibrating. Here was a middle aged salesperson trembling just because he was opening a message from his boss' boss.

The message was simple. It was an automated appointment. Mike Anderson expected Ed to be in his office Thursday morning at 7:30. Simply by clicking on the "Accept" button, Ed would be agreeing to an event that could well end his career with IVC.

This was Tuesday morning and Ed would have to sweat out the next forty-eight hours not knowing what the purpose or the outcome of that meeting might be.

As competitive as Ed was, his first thought was to bring in some sales as quickly as possible. Even if he could only gain some letters of commitment, maybe the company would give him a reprieve – a little more time to bring up his sales. The clock was ticking; Ed had to move, he had to move fast and he had to be successful.

His first action was to click the "Accept" button.

CHAPTER TWO: THE PROPOSAL

Ed immediately went to work looking at the proposals he had sent out and the initial contacts he had made over the past few weeks. Proposals were the most promising for him since they were the best opportunities for some immediate real successes.

Proposals were one of the last steps in the sales cycle. After getting a lead, Ed would do his initial analysis to determine the viability of the lead and then prioritize it based on the other leads he had. Then he would do his pre-call planning, set an appointment with the potential client and go out for the initial needs analysis. Depending on what he learned during the first interview, Ed would decide how to respond to the prospect – in person, in media or by electronic communication.

> 00:00
> **Pre-call planning is the first activity seasoned salespeople abandon**

This was Ed's sweet spot, or so he thought. Based on the data gathered in the needs analysis, Ed could structure a response that addressed the customer's problems, show them how IVC's solution could help them and he could expertly quantify IVC's value. If necessary, he was also prepared to demonstrate the superiority of the IVC solution over that of any other provider. If the customer was shopping, Ed could handle it.

> 00:00
> **Successful companies are shortening their sales cycles. It's one way to be fast.**

Depending on the complexity of the sale, the sales cycle could take up to six or seven months. From the time Ed got the lead until the time the customer signed the contract, time would be invested in responding to the customer's inquiries, demonstrating IVC's capabilities and superiority and then waiting for the client to work through their decision-making process.

Looking over the outstanding proposals, Ed hoped at least one of them would be close to closing.

As he scanned through the documents on his screen, Ed noticed how similar many of them were. Ed had developed a formula for success. About the time he was planning his trip to Acapulco, Ed had found that most of his sales fell into five or six categories. He could conduct a needs analysis and, within a short period of time, see that the client's issues fell into one of those categories.

Using Word and PowerPoint templates he had developed, Ed was able to respond quickly and thoroughly to the opportunities. Using cut-and-paste, his knowledge of the industry and the competition, he put together some powerful, attractive proposals.

The problem was they weren't closing.

There was no time to rework and resubmit the proposals. Ed would need to work as fast as he could to follow up with his client contacts.

His concentration was broken by Bubba Johnson. His real name was Robert, but the people in the Atlanta sales office called him Bubba and he seemed to like it. Bubba never met a stranger. He was one of those gregarious people who could strike up a conversation with anyone at anytime. He always had a joke ready even if some people found his humor inappropriate or even distasteful. For some reason, he talked louder than most other people.

> **00:00**
> Stop people at random and ask them to describe a salesperson and most will give an unflattering description . We don't enjoy an enviable reputation in most places.

Some people could not stand to be around him but no one could deny his success. He had closed more contracts than anyone else that year and everyone assumed he was on his way to being one of the top producers in the company. He might even match Ed's previous success. In fact, whenever he stepped into Ed's cubicle, he would point to the picture of Ed and Katherine in Acapulco and say, "Hey, that'll be me this year – think your wife would want to go with me? You could baby sit my old lady!" He would laugh as he walked out, not realizing how offensive and crude he was.

Ed was hoping Bubba would stay away this morning; he was in no mood to humor the boor. He also disliked the fact that he represented the same company as someone like Bubba.

There were nearly fifty outstanding proposals – a number that surprised Ed. He took the most promising one and called his contact. After a few rings the call went into voice mail and Ed's contact's voice greeting was, "This is Andy. I'll be at the sales meeting all this week; leave a message at the tone." Ed left a message and quickly moved on to the next proposal on his screen.

> 00:00
> Isn't it amazing how productive we can become in a crisis? Consider creating an artificial one for yourself...

After several calls, leaving voice messages on office and mobile phones, Ed finally succeeded in actually talking to someone. Roger Barrister from Baker Industries took his call and the world immediate began looking brighter.

"Ed," Roger said, "you were on my list to call today. We need to talk. I think Baker is ready to make a decision and I just need a few answers for us to move forward. Are you available on Thursday?"

Ed thought for a moment. Of course he could be available on Thursday but that would be after his meeting with the CSO, Mike Anderson. He might not be an employee of IVC by then.

"Actually, tomorrow would be much better for me, Roger. How does the day look for you?" Ed tried not to sound desperate.

"Tomorrow's jammed with plant tours," Roger answered. "Some people are coming in around nine and they will pretty much take the whole day. Hey, if you could come in around seven, I know it's early, but I have to be here at six-thirty to sign some papers. I could meet with you then."

"I'll be there!" Now Ed was trying not to sound too eager. "What questions should I be prepared to answer, Roger?"

"Mostly logistics. We will need the units shipped in lots of four or six and some will need to be drop-shipped to our outlying facilities. We need to know the units will be where we need them when we need them."

This is no problem for IVC. The operations facility had been undergoing something called "Lean Manufacturing" for a couple of years. They had recently conducted a Kaizen event, part of the Lean process, for the shipping department and now their shipments were "9/9": 99% accurate fill rate and 99% on time.

He thanked Roger for his time and hung up the phone. Only then did Ed notice the details of the proposal. Once again his cursor was vibrating

7

but this time it was excitement. The Baker Industries proposal had been out for nearly a year, had undergone several revisions and had been approved by both legal departments. All that was needed was for the budget to be approved and apparently that was done. The sale would be just under two million dollars over the next eighteen months. Ed's annual quota was $1.4 million. With a sale like this, Ed would be back: back on track for his quota and back on track for sales recognition.

Ed looked at the clock and saw that it was nearly one o'clock. With the pressure off, he decided to go to The Pub for his favorite lunch of fish and chips. He even considered going out for a round of golf in the afternoon to unwind and prepare for the big call he would be making in the morning.

Instead, he returned to the office after a leisurely lunch and made attempts to contact other clients who were sitting on proposals. He connected with a few, all of whom said they were not ready to make a decision, and left voice mails for the others.

He did leave the office a bit early, around four thirty, and took Katherine out for dinner.

CHAPTER THREE: THE CALL

Ed was up before four AM. He would need to leave his house around six to insure he was at Roger Barrister's office at Baker Industries on time. It was only a thirty to forty minute drive and there should not be that much traffic at that time of day but Ed had learned from experience that early is better than "too late".

Sitting in his car in front of the Baker Industries headquarters building at six forty, Ed had some time to review the account and to develop his strategy. He wished he had printed some of the notes from his computer and brought them with him. But he had a copy of the proposal and he knew Baker as well as he knew any of his accounts. After all, he had been working on this sale for a year before sending out the proposal and that was a year ago. "In two years you really get to know an account," he thought to himself.

> 00:00
> No matter how long we have been serving an account or how many times we've interacted with them, there are things we don't know. What we don't know can hurt us.

Baker Industries is an old school company so Ed was wearing a conservative suit and tie. He hardly wore ties anymore since selling in the high tech sector usually meant selling to younger whiz kids in jeans with their dog under their desk. A seasoned sales professional like Ed knows that you dress for the customer. This customer had a business dress code and Ed was appropriately attired.

Ed gathered up his papers, said a prayer under his breath and opened the car door.

There was no receptionist in Baker's lobby that early in the morning. Just as Ed was trying to decide what to do, Roger appeared on the other side of the glass door that led to the hallway. He smiled broadly and waved at Ed as he used his ID card to unlock and open the door.

"Come in, early bird!" Roger was in his usual good mood. Ed could not remember ever seeing Roger upset or anything but cheerful. If only all clients could be like him!

"Roger thanks for taking time to see me." Ed was making his way through the door as Roger held it open for him. "Looks like you're pulling some long hours too."

"Yes," Roger said, "we have clients in from New Jersey this morning and from the west coast this afternoon. It happens that way, sometimes. Want some coffee?"

"Is the Pope a Catholic? Of course I do!"

Both men chuckled and made their way into the kitchen. After pouring their coffee and making small talk, Roger guided Ed to the hallway and down to his office.

This was it. The big sale.

The two men sat at the small, round conference table in Roger's office. Ed was trying not to appear anxious or too nervous even though this was a huge sale. He decided to immediately address Roger's questions.

"Our operations department, as you know, is a Lean organization. What you may not know is that our shipping department has also undergone a Lean reorganization – an extreme makeover, if you will – and they are right now running 9/9." Ed saw Roger's face light up. "What that means is that we are hitting 99% accuracy in our order fill rate and also making 99% of our shipments on time." Ed was impressed with how smoothly the words were flowing out of his mouth.

He continued, "What this means for Baker is that we will have the units you want in the quantities you need at the locations you specify exactly when you need them."

Ed was surprised that Roger had become as serious as he had. Maybe it was just his business face, he thought.

"As soon as we have the contract in place, we will ask you for a delivery schedule with dates, parts and locations. We will enter that into our system and your equipment will be onsite like clockwork." Ed was using the subliminal technique of referring to his products as the customer's equipment. The customer would see Ed's company as the source of the equipment they would own.

Ed paused and waited for Roger to respond. It seemed to take Roger a long time, but that how it is in a situation like this. Time seems to stand still.

"Let me make sure I understand, Ed." Roger was looking at a map on the wall behind Ed. "IVC has gone through a Lean implementation and has only improved its performance to the 99% level? Most Lean organizations, like ours, use "9/9" to mean 99.9% order accuracy and a 99.9% fill rate. It sounds like IVC is fairly new to the Lean game. We will be placing 100, maybe even up to 300 orders per month. With a 99% accuracy rating we will experience one to three incorrect orders each month. I'm not sure we can afford that."

Ed was stunned. His greatest selling point of the day had just been dulled to point of being useless.

Roger continued, "Let's set that aside for a moment, Ed. We may be able to live with IVC's performance – after all, you're one of the best in your industry. I'm curious about which shippers you will use for ANWR and for Costa Rica. Will you be using your own trucks in those areas or will you rely on common carriers?"

> 00:00
> There is no such thing as having too much information; there is such a thing as giving too much

Suddenly Ed was hearing Greek. What was ANWR? Why were shipments needed to Costa Rica?

Sensing Ed's questions, Roger asked, "You know we just got the Mobil Oil contract, right? For all of their exploratory team communications? It's a two billion dollar deal for us. It's been in the papers. Hell, it's all over our web site. It's the biggest thing we've ever done."

> 00:00
> It's easier for senior salespeople to make rookie errors than it is for rookies

Ed was now associating with the deer in the headlights.

He had no idea of how IVC could – or even would – deliver to those areas. He had not been to Baker's web site in weeks. There was no finessing this one. He was caught. And before he knew it, he was out.

Leaving the building had been a blur. He vaguely remembered Roger saying something about getting some details back to him. And he thought Roger was cordial, maybe even smiling, as they shook hands when he left. But he could not be sure.

> 00:00
> The person at the table who knows the most about the other person's business wins

After sitting in his car for a while – he could not remember how long – Ed decided he needed to leave the customer's parking lot. Employees were coming to work. Other vendors were parking in the spaces reserved for vendors and he needed to leave.

He had made the worst rookie errors ever. No wonder his sales were sliding. He had lost his touch.

On the way back to the office, Ed pulled into a Starbucks. Maybe some caffeine and some comfort food would cheer him up.

He could not bring himself to get out of the car so he backed out to head back to the office. He had been so preoccupied with his situation that he failed to notice the car behind him.

CHAPTER FOUR: THE ENCOUNTER

The thud was not dramatic, but it was unmistakable. Ed got out of his car, assessed the damage and apologized profusely to the other driver. Ed's car was virtually untouched since his rear bumper had made most of the contact. The other car, however, had a huge dent in the front passenger door.

"I am so sorry," Ed said as the driver of the other car got out.

"It happens." The middle-aged gentleman was smiling and did not seem to be too upset. "Hey, nobody died and cars can be fixed." He was staring intently into Ed's eyes.

After a moment, Ed looked down and said, "I'm having one of the worst days of my life."

The man continued staring at Ed for a moment and then said, "You need some coffee and I need your insurance information. Let's go inside – my treat!"

Both men parked their cars and walked inside together. Ed stuck out his hand and said, "I'm Ed."

"Larry," said the gentleman. They walked over to the counter and Larry said, "A grande latte extra hot for me and whatever my friend here needs." He handed the cashier a Starbucks card and both he and the cashier waited for Ed.

"Just a medium coffee, please. Thank you."

Sitting at the table, Ed told Larry everything. He did not know why he was spilling all this out to a total stranger, but he could not help himself.

When he would stop talking, Larry would ask another question and he would become "motor mouth" again.

After nearly twenty minutes, Larry looked at Ed and asked, "Can I ask you a question?"

"Sure."

"Would you give me three, maybe five, adjectives that describe me?" Larry was smiling.

Ed was thinking that this was the most bizarre question he had ever been asked. He had just met this man and now the man wanted Ed's perception of him. Was he crazy? Was he a con man of some sort? What was he up to?

Larry's smile was genuine and reassuring so Ed answered. "Well, you're a good listener, obviously. And you seem to be intelligent. And I think you're a nice guy."

"What else?" Larry asked.

"You're a genuinely caring person, I think, and you are successful." Ed was stretching here.

"Which one of these descriptions would you like for your customers to use in describing you?"

Ed thought for a moment and answered, "All of them."

"Good," Larry was laughing now and leaning back in his chair. "What have we been talking about since we sat down?"

Ed immediately understood what Larry was saying. "I see. The more we talked about me, the more I appreciated you."

"Exactly," Larry said and then asked, "what is everyone's favorite subject?"

Ed thought for a moment, smiled, and said, "Themselves."

> 00:00
> What is every-
> one's favorite
> topic?

14

Larry took a long sip on his drink and said, "I need a refill. Get you anything?"

"No, thanks," Ed said.

After a few moments Larry returned to the table and said, "Okay, I need your insurance information."

Ed pulled out his wallet and handed his insurance card to Larry. Larry carefully copied the necessary information onto the back of one of his business cards and handed the insurance card back to Ed.

"Could I have one of your cards?" Ed asked.

"Sure, I'll swap with you – give me one of yours."

"Don't you want to call the police for an accident report?" Ed asked.

"No. I'm an insurance agent; my son owns a body shop so this is pretty straight forward for me. Your insurance company will call you in a day or two and ask if you really backed into me. It's pretty simple."

"What if I tell them I didn't do it?" Ed asked.

"If I thought you were that type of person I would have called the police."

00:00
Good salespeople use knowledge; great salespeople learn to balance knowledge and intuition

Ed thought for a minute and then asked, "So, as a fellow salesperson, you size up people, make a quick decision about them and then act on your intuition?"

"Well, intuition, being a good judge of character, or whatever you want to call it. It helps. But it isn't enough. We sell to everyone differently based on who they are and how they like to be sold. That's the intuitive part. After that, it becomes more of a scientific process based on knowledge and experience." Larry was trying to make a point but Ed was not getting it.

By this time Ed's mind was back on the problem at hand: his lack of sales. He became anxious to go back to his office to see if there might be another pending sale he could address.

He thanked Larry again, promised to keep in touch and got into his car. As he did, the disappointment of the morning sales call flooded back over him. By the time he reached the IVC headquarters building, he was jittery and irritable.

After an unproductive hour at his cubicle Ed was ready for a break. He took the elevator down to the cafeteria, picked out a small salad and found a table off by itself. He placed his tray on the table and walked over to the drink station to fill his glass.

A familiar face was there, a man refilling his own glass. He looked at Ed and his whole face lit up. "Ed! Ed! It's me – Charlie, Charlie Watkins – from the Teletronics class in Albany."

Teletronics was a new product line when Ed had been sent to Albany to learn all of the technical capabilities of the line. There he had met Charlie, an engineer from St. Louis. The two had been paired by the instructor to work on case studies together. Working on the exercises and sharing a few meals together had forged a bond between them. Three or four years had passed and Ed had forgotten his old classmate but, fortunately for him, Charlie had not forgotten him.

Charlie followed Ed back to his table and the two men began talking about the time in Albany. It took Ed's mind off of his problem for the moment. And it would prove to be one of the most important and productive conversations of Ed's sales career.

Ed was about to learn one of the most advanced selling processes from someone who had never held a sales position in his life.

CHAPTER FIVE: KAIZEN

Charlie Watkin's career had been exceptional. He was now the general manager over one of IVC's most advanced and sophisticated manufacturing facilities. He had been recognized as IVC's GM of the Year two years in a row, something that had never happened before.

"So what brings you here from St. Louis, Charlie?" Ed was beginning to remember how much he enjoyed working with Charlie. He stabbed more of his salad, lifted it to his mouth and waited for Charlie's answer.

"The brass wants to know more about Kaizen." Charlie watched Ed's eyes for a reaction. He wanted to see if he knew anything about the subject. "Are you familiar with Kaizen and Lean, Ed?"

"I thought I was but my client set me straight this morning." Ed did not want to relive the disastrous call. "What is it, really?"

"Kaizen is a Japanese word that means, generally, 'continuous improvement'. The Kaizen process is a formal, defined series of steps that leads to a reduction in time and cost of production."

"How does it work?" Ed was not really interested but wanted to hold up his side of the conversation. And he wanted to talk about anything other than his situation.

> **00:00**
> Whatever improvement programs - productivity, quality, etc. – that are being used in other parts of the organization need to be used in sales as well

"Well, it's simple, but it's not easy." Charlie took a sip of his drink and continued. "The results are just unbelievable. We have seen cycle times – the actual time it takes to make something or do something – drop dramatically. We have seen cost savings in the thousands and hundreds of thousands of dollars. You look at each step that needs to be done and ask yourself and your teammates,

> **00:00**
> **Major improvements usually begin with small, even minute, events**

'how can we do this better, faster and at a lower overall cost?' Then you look at what you can do to improve your handoff to the next person or department."

Ed tried to show interest but he had never worked in manufacturing; he had always been a sales guy. Charlie was very energetic and his enthusiasm for Kaizen was contagious. So Ed continued to feign interest in the subject, even though his mind kept wandering back to his problem and the morning disaster.

It was not until Charlie got specific that Ed began listening intently.

"Okay, let's see how it might work for you folks in sales." Charlie pulled out a piece of paper from his shirt pocket and flipped it over to the side where there was no printing. He looked in his shirt pocket and paused before selecting one of three pens that were there. Then he leaned over the table and looked at Ed.

"Let's begin at the beginning. Where does your work begin? What's the first step for you when you're looking for another sale?" Charlie turned the paper long ways and drew a horizontal line from the left margin to the right.

"I call the prospect and set an appointment to go out and do what we call a needs analysis. I ask questions to find out what the customer wants or needs and then I develop a proposal and follow up on it. Sometimes I close it, some…"

Charlie interrupted him. "Whoa, not so fast. Let's see," Charlie was looking at the line he had drawn and moving his pen from left to right along it. He placed his pen in the center of the page, drew a dot on the line and below the dot wrote "Call prospect".

> **00:00**
> **Salespeople often take too much for granted and can easily overlook the obvious**

Staring at the dot and with the pen touching his lips, Charlie asked, "How do you know who to call?"

"What do you mean?" asked Ed.

"Well," Charlie continued, "you call a prospect – how do you know who they are, what their phone number is and anything else about them?"

"We get our leads from marketing. Usually they are leads they picked up at trade shows. You know, people come by our booth, our people get their cards and then we follow up with them." Ed took another sip of his drink. This was routine stuff for him.

"Okay, so marketing hands you a bunch of leads they got at a trade show. Do they just give you a stack of business cards?"

"No, actually it's a print out. It has columns for the person's name, title, company, email and phone – things like that."

"And does every lead turn into a sale?"

Ed heard himself laugh. "No, no my friend. Actually only a few ever result in a sale. Sales is a numbers game." Ed took another sip from his drink. "If I get, say, one hundred leads, there may be three or four sales there. Occasionally one of those will develop into a good account but most of them go

> 00:00
> **Managing the sales funnel means that we find ways of increasing the number of leads that result in sales**

nowhere. It's called the sales funnel because there are more opportunities coming in the top than there are sales coming out the bottom."

"Why is that?" Charlie asked.

"Well, first of all, the leads are usually several weeks old by the time I make the call. Most of the people have to be reminded of what they saw at our booth. Sometimes they have to be reminded that they ever went to the show. These leads are so cold that they're not really worth a lot."

Charlie was drawing another dot on his line. This time it was at the left margin of the piece of paper. He labeled the dot "Leads" and below it wrote "cold" and circled the word. "So you need warm leads, not cold leads? You have a supplier who is giving you inferior products, ones that do not meet your needs. Right?"

"I guess you could say that. It's just the way it is. Nothing can be done about that – it's always been that way."

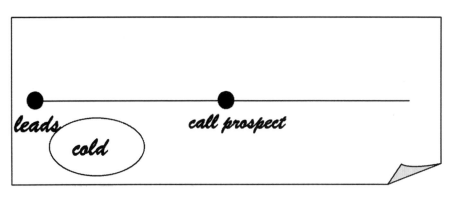

Now Charlie was grinning broadly.

"What's so funny?" Ed asked.

"That is one of the primary and most obvious targets for Kaizen: the idea that something cannot be improved. The way it was is not the way it needs to be and, therefore, it <u>must</u> change." Neither man spoke for a moment. The Charlie asked, **"What would it take to keep the lead warm until you can make the call?"**

"Figure that out, Charlie, and you'll be the best friend of every salesperson here." Ed looked at his watch, his face soured and he said, "Look, it was great seeing you again, Charlie. Let's stay in touch. I need to get back upstairs."

> **00:00**
> **Thinking through the situation and then asking the hard questions is the beginning of the solution**

The two men shook hands and walked towards the counter to throw away their cups. Charlie pointed to a stainless steel drawer that was built in the counter below the area that held the utensils and condiments and asked, "What's that?"

"It's a warming drawer. Sometimes the cafeteria will have bread in there. It keeps the bread warm. It's better that putting it in the microwave since the microwave changes the texture of the bread and makes it less appetizing."

Charlie placed his hand on Ed's shoulder. "So what you have in sales now is a microwave process to warm up those cold leads and what you need is a warming oven?"

Ed laughed; Charlie made a note on his piece of paper.

CHAPTER SIX: THE MEETING

Wednesday afternoon produced no real results for Ed and Wednesday night brought little sleep. With the looming meeting Thursday morning, Ed was even more restless and irritable than he had been.

As he dressed for work Thursday morning, Katherine brought him a steaming cup of coffee and placed it on the dresser.

"You are a very talented man who is just entering the best years of his life. You have a lot to give, Ed. If IVC cannot see it and appreciate it, there are companies out there who can. The right opportunity is waiting for you and this is the path that will take you there." There was no mistaking the sincerity and the energy behind her words.

Ed did not look at her, so she spoke again. "We have weathered a lot worse than this, Ed. This will be the beginning of something new and grand. I know it to be so."

> **00:00**
> **Who are the encouragers in your life – the people who put courage in you?**

Ed knew that when Katherine used those exact words, "I know it to be so", it had a deep meaning for her. Ed wanted what she had said to be true. And, he wanted today to be over.

When Ed pulled into the parking lot a little after seven, there were only a few cars there. One was Mike Anderson's. Ed looked up and saw that the light was on in Mike's office on the third floor. Like a man going to the gallows, Ed tried to walk with pride but it was difficult.

Ed went through his morning routine of turning on the coffee maker, logging in to pull down his emails and then pouring himself a cup. The usual emails came in, the morning Sales Status report showed Ed less than half-way up the list. It also showed Bubba at the number two slot. This is not the company that it was when he joined, Ed thought.

An appointment reminder popped up on Ed's screen with the usual chirping sound. Ed knew it was time to face his fate. "Mike Anderson, CSO, 7:30 AM."

Mike Anderson's outer office was empty. No one was there to announce his arrival so Ed attempted to make some innocent-sounding noises to let Mike know he was waiting. It wasn't necessary. Mike appeared in the doorway to his office, reached out his hand and with a seemingly genuine smile ushered Ed inside.

"I see you brought your own coffee – do you need it topped off? Want some water?" Mike was being very accommodating. Maybe this was like a condemned man's last meal, Ed thought.

In some ways Mike's office was like any of the others on Mahogany Row. (There was no Mahogany; the term was a throwback to the original executive offices back in New York.) The office was spacious, had the usual desk, credenza sofa, chair and coffee table. What was different was that Mike had three computers driving a total of seven screens. Some screens were changing continuously, like a stock market monitor. Others changed more slowly and some merely had blinking indicators.

"Have a seat," Mike said, gesturing towards the sofa. It was the oldest positioning trick in the book. The power seat is the single chair; the subservient seat is the sofa. Ed knew that Mike was playing the power game.

Ed sat down and waited to hear how Mike would open the meeting. Would he talk about the family and ask about Katherine? Did he even remember meeting her in Acapulco? This would be a tactic to soften up Ed. Would he open with a question about how Ed saw his current level of performance? That was usually the loaded question, the one the power player would use to hang the weaker player – it was referred to as the noose. Maybe he would use the term "another direction", a phrase that means we're going this way and you're going that way. Ed had played through these scenarios as he lay in bed the night before unable to sleep.

> **00:00**
> "Noose questions" are questions that have enough rope in them to allow us to hang ourselves

"So, how's it going upstairs, Ed?" It was a noose question. Ed was prepared for it.

"You know it's been better, it will soon be better again and right now it's a struggle. Tough times toughen us up for the good times." It was mostly platitudes but it served its purpose.

"Ed, sales is changing. It is changing fast and the changes are permanent. We have to take our sales process, our sales focus and everything else about our selling to the next level. We have to move in another, untried direction. Once we arrive there, it will be time to change again."

00:00
Thoughts and emotions have physical manifestations

There was the phrase, "another direction". Ed's coffee began tasting bitter all of a sudden.

Mike pointed to his desk area and said, "You see those screens over there? That is how I must make decisions now. There is less and less room for error. There is virtually no time for mistakes because there is no time for 'do-overs.'" Mike took a sip of his coffee and continued.

"It used to be that we could introduce a new product or program and it would take the competition a year to catch up. By then we would have moved on to the next new thing. Today, in a matter of only a few weeks, they will be touting their 'me too' product or program. Differentiations do not last. Technology is readily available to anyone who wants it. Our best chance at success now is our sales team. We have to tell a different message, we have to tell it quickly and, at the same time, we have to hold down our sales costs." Mike picked up a booklet from the coffee table. "That's where you come in, Ed."

00:00
Differentiations do not last long anymore

What was the booklet? Was it Ed's severance package? Was it a guide to writing a good resume? All Ed could read was three large letters on the cover: "R.S.A."

"Ever heard of Real Sales Automation, Ed?" Mike asked?

"I don't think so." Ed answered.

"I hadn't either until a couple of months ago. It is going to help IVC significantly improve our sales performance. It is not a cure-all, it's not a panacea, but it is an important part of the new sales dynamic."

00:00
RSA goes far beyond
the use of a CRM

Mike continued, "Like every other company, including our competitors, we have implemented a Client Relationship Manager program and we have one of the best CRM's available. It is not enough. We have implemented an ERP system to keep all departments on the same page of the same songbook at the same time. That's critical, even mandatory, but it's not enough. We are aggressively implementing the principles and techniques of Kaizen everywhere in the company. That is, everywhere except sales and that is about to change.

"Are you familiar with Kaizen, Ed?"

Talk about luck. The chance meeting with Charlie the day before in the cafeteria was proving to be a real stroke of luck.

"It means, uh, continuous improvement or something like that, right?"

"Exactly!" Mike was animated now. "So at least you are aware of the concept. We are going to bring the strengths and advantages of Kaizen into the sales force and I am looking for a champion – someone who will spearhead the project. Are you interested?"

Ed's head was spinning now. He needed a moment to collect his thoughts. Thank goodness for coffee cups. Ed took a long sip and found that the bitterness was gone from the coffee.

"I'm interested; I just don't know anything about Kaizen, especially Kaizen for Sales."

"That's the beauty of this – nobody does. At least, nobody I can find. There are few books and programs out there and the ones that exist do not exactly fit our unique needs. We need to figure this out, Ed, and I think you're the person to take this on."

"But why me?" Ed asked. "How did you choose me?"

"I didn't; Number 5 did."

"Who is Number 5?" Ed was curious.

Mike pointed to the screens on his desk. "We are using sales analytics which involve a number of software programs. Each of those screens is numbered – see the number on the upper left corner? Screen number five came back and told me you were the right guy. I decided what my criteria was, typed it in and, about one nanosecond later, screen number five gave me your name."

"Really? What were your criteria?"

"I wanted a seasoned sales professional who understands what is involved in sales. I also wanted someone who understood technology. If I could find someone who had succeeded and failed in sales, someone who was already making use of the CRM and other tools – and doing it well – that would be the ideal candidate.

"Frankly I was surprised to see your name pop up."

"Why?"

"You know Bruce Denlow in the Chicago office?"

"Yes, we met in Acapulco. He is a consistent high performer. I think he's the one who has made the President's Club the most often, right?"

"That's right, Bruce is a consistent winner. He has not experienced a bad year in a long time which makes him the wrong guy for this job. He does not remember what it feels like to lose or what causes slumps. He does not know where the weaknesses in the system are because he never experiences them. And besides, he's making too much money where he is."

> 00:00
> We often learn more through our failures than our successes

Mike peered into his now empty cup and asked, "More coffee?"

The two men walked down the hall to the executive kitchen and re-filled their cups. Mike explained that the RSA project would be a two or three year endeavor and might become a permanent position. Ed would report directly to Mike and would be a part of a team that would include an experienced Kaizen implementer and would have access to the IT department to build whatever sales automation tools were necessary.

"We're interviewing for the Kaizen position right now. We like Charlie Watkins from St. Louis – do you know him?"

Ed smiled. It was not coincidence that he and Charlie had linked up earlier. "Yes, he and I attended a two-week school in Albany. I saw him yesterday – he's a real evangelist for Kaizen."

"See if you can direct some of that energy and knowledge Charlie has towards the sales side of the house will you?" Mike paused. "I'm assuming here that you will take the position, right?"

> **00:00**
> New and challenging opportunities are "fun" for successful people

Ed paused a moment, looked down at the floor, and then answered. "I think this will be fun!" There was a level of energy back in his voice that had been missing for a long time.

Then Mike said, "Okay, not a word of this to anyone. I need to talk to Linda and let her talk to Rick before we announce this. Right now this is just between the two of us." Linda Colburn was the Vice President of Ed's division and Rick Harper was Ed's regional manager. They would need to be informed from the top down.

On the elevator going up to the sales floor, Ed was suddenly drained. The emotion and tension from the past two days finally caught up with him. If there was any way he could leave early, he would. He wanted to make a quick call to Katherine as soon as he got to his cubicle but since the information was secret for now, he would have to find a conference room or, maybe go outside.

It was not to be. When he walked into his cubicle, his voice mail light was already flashing. More importantly, there was a hand-written note on his phone that said, "My office NOW! – Rick".

CHAPTER SEVEN: QUESTIONS

The rule is that when you take your best salesperson and make them a sales manager, you get two things: less sales and bad management. There was an exception to that rule. Rick Harper was an effective Regional Manager. He had been one of the top-producing salespeople who had made the successful leap to sales management. Most great salespeople do not make great managers.

Some people who worked for Rick found him to be too blunt and too pushy. There was no arguing with the numbers his teams produced. Whatever his style, Rick had built and managed one strong team after another.

He was also known to be a man of few words – another break from the typical image of a salesperson.

Ed knew from experience that a note like the one he had from Rick needed to be his top priority.

Walking over to Rick's office, Ed assumed the conversation would be about his numbers. The morning report showed Bubba moving very close to the top slot and Ed inching in the other direction. Ed's numbers had been down all year, why the sudden urgency from Rick? His note had the word "NOW" was written in large letters.

> **00:00**
> Effective salespeople modify their behavioral and communications styles to improve the customer's ability to hear and understand the message

Everyone in the Atlanta sales office had been trained on the DISC system for recognizing and interacting with different behavioral styles. Rick was a hard-charging "D", what some people refer to as the Type A personality. Ed was a high "I" or intuitive type of person which is common among salespeople. Ed's second suit was "D" and so he would shift into the D mode whenever he talked with Rick – especially today.

This behavioral shift came naturally and easily for Ed since he had been using it for so many years.

People who have not been in sales will often see this behavior shift as insincerity, as the salesperson being a chameleon and changing just to meet whatever style the customer responded to. It was true. Effective salespeople modify their behavior to better match the behavior their customer appreciates. They do not compromise their ethics or integrity nor do they alter their price just to make a sale. They do, however, present their offering in a way that is most effective for the customer.

Knowing that the new position was in the works, Ed was not too worried about the encounter. He would soon be leaving the rank-and-file sales role he had been playing and would move into the new sales Kaizen position. He did not think anything Rick would say would bother him. Any discussion of his poor performance would be moot now.

He was wrong.

"What happened at Baker Industries yesterday? Rick was seated at his desk, shuffling through some papers as he asked the question.

Ed was stunned. He had not completed a call report on the disastrous call yet – how would Rick know about it?

"Well, uh, I..." Ed stammered. Being unable to formulate a cohesive was unfamiliar territory for him. He was usually better on his feet than this. He took a deep breath and started again.

"I blew it. I assumed they were ready to sign. I had talked with Roger Barrister the day before, asked about his objections and went in prepared to address them. He came out of left field with some questions I was not prepared to answer."

Ed paused to see if this was enough for Rick. It wasn't.

"So, I am developing a response now and plan to get the sale back on track." Ed remembered that Rick wanted the facts. No stories, facts. Rick would also expect concrete, measurable tactics so he added, "I will have that done by tomorrow and I will get back with Roger the first of next week."

As soon as he heard the words come out of his mouth, he knew he had made a mistake.

Rick asked, "What is keeping you from developing a response today and meeting with him this afternoon or tomorrow? Do we really want him stewing over the weekend?"

"You're right. I will get on it right away and have it done before I leave. I'll find out when I can get on his calendar – tomorrow if at all possible."

"You've been working this project for a long time, Ed, how did you find yourself in this position?" Rick was staring at Ed now. There was no identifiable expression on his face so Ed could not tell what Rick was thinking.

"Apparently," Ed said, "they closed a contract with Mobil that is significant for them and I was not aware of it."

Rick paused and continued staring for what seemed like minutes to Ed and then asked, "Don't you read the Papers? When was the last time you went to their site?"

Ed was caught. In his sales slump he had become lazy. He was not reading the trade journals as often and he certainly was not doing an effective job of pre-call planning.

> **00:00**
> Anyone can make a mistake – how you respond to it will determine your level of success

"Look, I blew it." Ed was pacing around Rick's office now.

Rick asked, "What are you doing to not blow the next call?

What a great question. Ed had been so busy licking his wounds that he had not begun to make the changes that would pull him out of his slump.

"I won't make any more customer visits without going to the client's web site."

"What about before returning a phone call or responding to an email?" Rick asked.

"Customers expect us to be responsive, Rick. I like to return phone calls and reply to emails immediately. We are supposed to be reacting fast, aren't we?"

> **00:00**
> **Fast does not necessarily mean immediate**

"Yes, of course, but does fast mean immediate?"

"What do you mean?" Ed stopped pacing and stared back at Rick.

"Our customers want a quality response and part of quality is speed – what is another part of quality?" Rick pulled a piece of paper out of his trash can and began making notes on the back of a memo he had received.

"Another part of quality? As it relates to returning phone calls? Well, I suppose having the information the customer needs when we contact them." Thinking back on the call the day before, Ed added, "and having the latest information as well."

> **00:00**
> **Taking notes as we talk is a powerful tool whether we are in front of a customer, friend, or anyone else**

"Good. How does doing some planning save time for the customer and for us?"

Ed thought for a moment and then answered, "Well, the customer does not have to take time to educate us on what we should already know."

"Okay, what else?"

"If we have access to their information, we should be able to answer their questions without having to call them back or make another visit."

"Anything else you can think of, Ed?"

"Hmmm, no. But I'm sure as soon as I leave your office I will think of a few!"

Both men smiled. Then Rick got serious. "Ed, you have fallen into the most common trap for seasoned salespeople. Do you know what that is?"

"Tell me," Ed said.

"Winging it. Seasoned salespeople begin winging their calls because they think they're so good they can tap dance around anything. Remember your first sales call?"

"Like it was yesterday."

00:00
A primary trap for seasoned salespeople is "winging it"

"How much time did you spend preparing for that call?"

"Days," Ed answered. "I practiced in a mirror, did some role play with my boss and developed a long series of questions."

"When did you decide you didn't need to do pre-call planning anymore?"

Ed sat down. "I don't know. I think I just evolved into it."

Rick was making notes on the piece of paper from his trash can as Ed answered. "So, if you had done some pre-call planning before going out to Baker, how would the call have changed?"

"Well," Ed began, "I would have told Roger that I knew about the Mobil contract and I would have told him about our relationships with the distributors who serve those faraway sites they will need to reach." Ed paused for a minute and then added, "Oh, and I would not have told him about our Kaizen initiative. Their's is so much stronger than ours."

Rick finished writing on the scrap paper, looked up at Ed and said, "Why is that the worst possible answer to that question?"

Now Ed was stumped. So, Rick continued, "Instead of telling the customer about something new in their business, what could you do?"

It was coming back to Ed now. "Oh, yeah. I should have _asked_. Instead of telling them what little I know, I should have asked a question that would have given me greater understanding of what they are doing."

00:00
Talking to customers can ruin relationships; asking questions can strengthen them

"Okay, what could you have asked Roger about Baker's Mobil contract?"

This was not getting any easier. Ed had to think for a moment before answering. "I could have, well, I guess I could have asked Roger what Mobil's expectations were. Maybe there is something else we could do to help Baker better serve Mobile! I see where you're going."

"Actually, you are seeing where you should have gone already, Ed. You're better than this. Now, what is the process for what you are describing?"

IVC conducted many sales training courses and covered various aspects of selling. It was hard to remember all of them. "Let me see," Ed answered, "oh yeah, Supply Chain Selling. 'Don't Sell To – Sell Through', right?" Help your customer sell more of their stuff and they'll buy more of yours."

"Good, Ed. Now what would you change about how you responded to Roger's question about the remote sites?"

> **00:00**
> Memorizing and internalizing sales nuggets, like "sell through, not to", is essential for keeping selling on track

"Well, let's see." Ed was looking at the floor. "Of course I could have asked what they wanted us to do – wait, wait, I could have asked what Mobil wanted from them at those sites."

"And what else?"

"What else? I don't know – what else could I have asked?"

"How about what additional remote sites Mobile would be opening up in the future?"

"Hey, that's good. It would have shown interest in the customer, in the customer's customer and it could have led to some vertical selling. But Monday morning quarterbacking is easier than being in the heat of the game, you know."

"You could have run the call by me or anyone else in the sales office, couldn't you? Wouldn't new ideas have come from those

> **00:00**
> Vertical selling is selling more products or services to existing clients. Horizontal selling is selling to new accounts

sessions? And isn't it possible that there are still some great ideas that you and I have not thought of?"

Rick let that thought sink in before continuing. "Okay, now, how would you have addressed the Kaizen issue differently?"

"Ed looked at Rick and said, "Like I said, I would not have brought it up?"

"Because...?" Rick asked.

"Well, because Baker Industries is better at it than we are. They use 9/9 to mean 99.9% accuracy and 99.9% fill rate. We use it to mean 99%. It makes us look bush league compared to them."

"Really?" Risk asked.

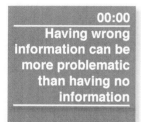

00:00

Having wrong information can be more problematic than having no information

Ed felt uncomfortable. He had no response for Rick's question so Rick asked another. "How do you know our use of 9/9 is not the same as Baker's?"

Try as he might, Ed could not remember where he had gotten his information. Had he misstated his own company's capabilities?

"Is there anyone here at the corporate headquarters of IVC who could explain our Kaizen initiative for you? Is that information on our web site?"

"What should I be doing differently, Rick?" Ed's hands were now in his lap and he leaned back into the chair.

"I don't know, what do you think?"

Ed took a quick inventory and then said, "I should go back to doing pre-call planning. I need to stay better informed about the customer and, I guess about us as well."

"You guess?" Rick interjected.

"No, you're right. I need to go back and review what our real strengths are."

"How will you do it?"

Ed leaned forward in his chair, thought for a while and then said, "Ask more questions. Ask more questions of more people."

"One more thing before you leave, Ed." Rick was smiling now. "Did you realize that everything I said to you today I said in the form of a question?"

"You were using Jeopardy Selling on me?"

"I sure was; did you feel like I was interrogating you?"

> 00:00
> Jeopardy Selling
> is phrasing every-
> thing in the form
> of a question

"Not at all. I felt like we were working together to solve a problem."

"Good, will you keep that in mind during you post-call critique?"

"You mean when I critique..." Ed was confused. "What post call critique?"

"Well, this one, of course. You were going to review our conversation, right?"

"Yes, I suppose."

"Formally or informally?"

"Yeah, I get it. I should sit down and do a post-call critique on every significant call, win or lose."

"You see, you do remember the training we gave you, don't you? Would you like a transcript or the audio?"

"What, what!?!" Ed's words came out of his mouth before he could stop them.

Rick held up a small, digital recorder. "A lesson you seem to have forgotten is to record every call and go back and review it. It is the most powerful and most effective sales coaching ever – remember?"[1]

---

1 *Note: in some circumstances recording a conversation without the permission of all parties can be a legal issue – check with counsel.*

Ed stood up, reached out to shake Rick's hand and asked, "Can you just send me the audio?"

> **00:00**
> The most powerful and effective sales development process is to record your sales calls and other conversations with customers and then go back and review the recording

"Finally, you asked a question!" Rick said. "Good luck with the Kaizen project, Ed."

"You know about that?"

"I asked around." Rick was now back to shuffling the papers on his desk.

CHAPTER EIGHT: KAIZEN 2

Ed left Rick's office, went by his cubicle, grabbed his mobile phone and headed outside. He walked around the building in the manicured lawn as he waited for Katherine to answer her phone. The warmth of the sun was making this day better and better. After explaining the events of the day, Ed said he needed to get back to work.

"See," Katherine said, "I told you that you have too much to offer. Way to go, champ."

He returned to his cubicle and began retrieving his voice mails and emails. Among the voice mails was an excited call from Charlie Watkins, the Kaizen expert from St. Louis. Did he know that he and Ed would be working together?

"I think I figured it out, Ed. It came to me this morning – give me a call as soon as you can." Charlie's voice was more animated than Ed would have thought.

After responding to some customer-related issues, Ed returned the call to Charlie.

"Hey, Charlie, it's Ed. What's up?"

"Well, I got to thinking about how the principles and techniques of Kaizen might help you sales guys. Remember, I don't know anything about sales, but hear me out."

Ed pulled out a piece of paper in case he needed to make notes.

"You said that the leads you were getting from marketing were old and cold by the time you got them. Some of the customers had forgotten who you are and what you offer, right?" Before Ed could answer, an excited

Charlie continued. "That's like a manufacturing cell getting a defective part from a supplier or from another cell – someone in our own organization. For instance, suppose the first step in a manufacturing operation was to cut one inch off of the pipe they received from the pipe supplier. Wouldn't it save time and money to have the pipe supplier ship shorter pieces of pipe?"

"Sure," Ed answered.

"Okay, you're getting leads that don't meet your standards. They're old and cold. You have to warm them up and rejuvenate them. What if marketing could keep them hot and interested until you could talk to them?"

"How would they do that?" Ed was curious. This was his first incursion into Kaizen for sales and he resisted the urge to tell Charlie that if it could be done, it would already be done.

"You indicated that when you got the lead, you had access to the information from their business card, right?"

Ed thought for a minute and said, "Yes. At the trade show, we take the person's card and scan it or we are able to scan their badge and we have their basic contact info. Sure."

> **00:00**
> How can technology help you sell more effectively?

"Okay, then why couldn't that information be used to send the customer a periodic reminder of who we are and what we do? Maybe they wouldn't forget us! We could send an e-newsletter or product brochures or something like that."

Ed knew the idea of an e-newsletter would not work because most people are receiving too many of them already. But he liked where Charlie was going.

"Since we would be in continuous communication with the customer, if they had a need before we contacted them, they would call us!"

Charlie was a bit naïve about sales. The customers, actually prospects in this case, would not necessarily call IVC. They would, however, be *more likely* to call.

"So, I came up with this scenario. Let's say that you and I go to a trade show – are you with me? We visit a booth and then call it a day and go back to our hotel rooms. What is the first thing we're going to do? Right, check our emails!"

Charlie was not waiting for answers to his questions, he was on a roll. Salespeople are like that sometimes, unfortunately, and right now Charlie was selling.

"You get an email that thanks you for dropping by the booth and talks about the salability of the product and I get an email that addresses the technical side. Get it? Based on our job title, we each receive different messages." Charlie was on a roll. "Okay, then, two days later we get another email with links on it. Depending on which link we click – or maybe even multiple links because we click on several, the vendor sends us information that is relevant for us. Are you with me?"

Ed nodded, even though he was on the telephone, Charlie apparently understood and continued, "This way your lead never gets cold. And if they need to buy, you're only a click away. I don't know web stuff but I know all of this can be done. What do you think?"

Since Charlie was taking a breath, Ed replied, "I think it sounds good. Anything that could keep our leads from going cold would be a good thing. Who else is doing this?"

"I don't know what other sales teams are doing. I don't even know what you guys are doing! I just heard you say this was a problem and I'm showing you a solution. Talk to you later – I need to run to a meeting."

Ed continued working, following up on sales in his pipeline and setting appointments. He had given himself one hour to touch other accounts before digging in and trying to save the Baker deal. Whenever he caught himself talking to a client, he would try to change his message to a question. It was working. **The more questions he asked, the more success he was having.**

> 00:00
> Non-sales people can often give us new insights

Although he had vowed to call Roger Barrister at Baker and set another appointment before leaving the office, his pre-call planning ate more time than he had expected. When he finished his planning, he looked up and it was dark outside. He would need to call Barrister in the morning.

By the time he completed his pre-call planning, Ed was thoroughly familiar with Baker Industry's web site as well as the web sites of Mobile, Baker's client, two of Baker's competitors and the web site of IASPI – the International Association of Suppliers to the Petroleum Industry. Ed had found the affiliation with IASPI on Baker's web site.

He was just about to leave the office when his phone rang. Ed picked up the receiver and noticed the time on his screen. It was 8:55 – he assumed the call would be from someone in another time zone.

It was Charlie.

"You dog! Why didn't you tell me? We're going to be working together on the sales Kaizen project." Charlie's voice was even more animated now than it had been earlier. "Looks like we'll be moving back to Atlanta – that will make my wife happy. Wow."

Ed spoke up, "Well, I did not know it was a done deal and I didn't know if I could talk about it. Sounds like they're serious and moving fast, right?"

"Yes,", Charlie answered, "We will need to do our first Kaizen event next week. I'm coming back on Monday; let's set it up for Tuesday. We will need a conference room for about three days – can you arrange that?"

"Next week? I have calls scheduled for next week. No, no, Charlie, I will need a couple of weeks to get things in order here. Besides, I haven't heard any official word on this yet." Ed's mind was racing.

"Obviously you haven't been around Kaizen. Things are about to start happening very fast in your life." Charlie paused a minute and then added, "I don't know much about sales and I haven't heard of a sales Kaizen event be-

> **00:00**
> **Make faster decisions**
> **– ready, fire, aim**

fore. We may be going into uncharted waters here. We are going to need to have some other people in the room for those three days. Let's see, we'll need three or four salespeople – good ones and bad ones – and we will need someone from marketing and it would help if someone from manufacturing could be there. Let's don't involve any engineers at this point."

Ed's life was definitely accelerating.

Ed hung up the phone and looked up to see his manager, Rick, standing in his cubicle. "Looks like you're on the rocket, my friend. I just got a call from downstairs. They have some office space set aside for the Kaizen initiative and I'm supposed to give your accounts to other reps."

Rick continued, "You're keeping one, however. Baker Industries." Rick waited to see how Ed would react. "That's a mess you're going to have to clean up. Let's see if this Kaizen stuff will do that!"

The gauntlet had been thrown down.

CHAPTER NINE: THE EVENT

A Kaizen event is a formal process that examines an entire process in the most minute detail. Once the process is laid out, each step, sub-step – even the most simple aspect – can be evaluated. The Kaizen event is then used to determine how to do that particular action better and faster.

IVC's first sales Kaizen event would begin on Tuesday.

Following Charlie's phone call on Thursday, things began happening quickly. Ed had gone to the third floor where he was shown the available office space. It had been used by a project team that was now completed and consisted of three closed-door offices, a medium sized conference room and a bull pen with a few cubicles.

> 00:00
> **Kaizen events need to be repeated for continuous improvement**

This would Ed's new home-away-from-home. At least he would have an office now, but the environment seemed cold and unfamiliar.

Ed used his day on Friday to shift his other accounts to other reps and to talk to some key accounts about the changes. He stalled before calling Roger Barrister at Baker.

Finally, he gathered up enough courage and placed the call. As soon as he heard Roger's voice, Ed tensed up unexpectedly but quickly composed himself. It had been a long time since he had felt this much tension in a call.

"Roger, thanks for taking my call." Ed began. "First of all, I want to apologize for being so unprepared Wednesday – there is no excuse for that, I was just lazy and I'm sorry."

Ed paused and waited to hear if Roger would respond. He didn't, so Ed continued, "Our delivery capabilities are on par with Baker's and in fact, according to the folks I talked to in shipping, we are going 'second decimal' and beginning to measure our performance to the 99.99% mark." Ed looked down at his notes and continued, "We have distributors in both ANWR and Costa Rica who are actually carrying most of the lines Baker uses right now and we will see that they stock the remaining ones."

Ed then pulled out information that he had pulled from Mobil's web site. "Best of all, Roger, we also have distributor relationships in Russia and in the Pacific Region. Since Mobil has announced they are going there as well, we can help Baker stay in front of their efforts."

Ed had nothing more to say, and realized he had downloaded statements instead of asking questions. Would he ever learn?

So Ed quickly formulated a question, "Roger, what would it take for IVC to get back into the game with Baker?"

> **00:00**
> When a question is on the table, the first person to speak usually loses

There was a long pause. Ed knew that who ever spoke first after the question is on the table loses.

Finally Roger answered, "You were never out of the game, Ed. I just needed more commitment from your side. This is a huge deal for us and we want IVC to want us to succeed as much as we do. Sounds like you're back in the game to me."

The two men agreed on a meeting to finalize the paperwork. Ed would determine how he would stay on top of the account as he moved into the new position and stay on top until Rick, his manager, decided to give responsibility to someone else.

The week had been the rockiest of Ed's career. He felt like he had been on an emotional roller coaster and now the week was ending better than any he could remember.

> **00:00**
> Success in sales and success at home go hand in hand

On the way home he would stop and pick up flowers for Katherine, a bottle of wine for celebration and a pint of Ben & Jerry's Cherry Garcia.

On Saturday he and Katherine went in to the office, packed up his belongings and went down to the new space. Katherine helped Ed decide which office he would use and together they set up his new environment. With Katherine's help, it actually seemed more homey and comfortable than his cubicle had.

Ed would begin work here on Monday and would help Charlie get settled in.

Sunday night Katherine called Ed into the kitchen. "Tomorrow is a big day for you," she began. "I don't want you distracted. So, the girls and I are meeting for breakfast at 7:30 and then we're going to play tennis. After that, I'm going to get my hair cut. Then I'm picking up Mother and taking her to an early dinner and out to see that movie she's been talking about. In other words, I'll be busy – don't even think about calling me unless absolutely necessary."

Katherine had learned that there is a limit to Ed's ability to multitask. That is true for everyone. She was smart enough to remove the one task element she could control. Ed did not know it at the time, but it was a Kaizen moment in their home.

On Monday morning Ed was awake early and decided to go in to the office and begin his new mission. He arrived in the parking lot just after six AM. He was alone.

Ed turned on the lights in the new space and walked to his new office. As soon as he sat down he realized something had changed. He walked to his door, and there it was. In the adjacent office was Charlie's belongings. Ed recognized Charlie in a picture with a woman and three children. He saw some of Charlie's framed documents on the wall.

"How did he do that?" Ed asked, though no one else was around.

Before seven that morning, Charlie was in the office with a steaming cup of coffee. "'Morning, Ed," he said cheerfully. "How was your weekend?"

"Busy – but obviously not as busy as yours. How did you get your stuff here from St. Louis so quickly? Where did you find the time? And where did you get the coffee?"

Charlie smiled. "Come on, I'll show you." Charlie walked briskly, something Ed would need to match. They walked across the building to

Mahogany Row, Charlie pushed open the door and the two men walked in.

"You're drinking the brass' coffee?" Ed would never have considered doing this.

"In a lean organization, Ed, everything is lean. The brass knows that we're going to drink coffee, they know that only resource on this floor is here in their kitchen and if we have to go upstairs for coffee it will waste a lot of time."

> **00:00**
> Respect for authority and hierarchy are not challenged by incidental activities like sharing coffee pots

Back in Ed's office Charlie said, "We're in luck. I thought we would have to invent the process for sales Kaizen – it turns out some of the work has been done for us already."

Charlie took a sip of his coffee and continued, "I Googled the topic and found a web site, _KaizenForSales.com._ Here is what they suggest. Instead of using post-it notes to list each step in order, use PowerPoint or Word – and they explain how."

"Post-it notes?" Ed asked.

"Yeah," Charlie answered, "we used to write each step on a Post-it note and stick them on the wall around the room. That way we could see the whole process laid out. There is a way to use Word instead, I played with it last night in my hotel, and I think it'll work just fine."

Ed nodded. He was not really following what Charlie was saying but he trusted that he knew what he was talking about.

Charlie continued, "Here is the best part. They suggested that we list every step involved in what they called the sales cycle..." Charlie interrupted himself, "Do you know what they're talking about?"

"Yes, of course – I'll explain it in a minute, keep going."

"Once the sales cycle is laid out, then we will map the sales process. They define the sales process as each step in each element of the sales cycle. Does that make sense?"

Ed answered, "Yes, I think so. I'm with you so far."

Charlie leaned forward, "Okay, here's the good part. This is the part I didn't get because it was sales and I don't know much about sales. They say that we look at each step in the sales process and apply the EDA Factor."

"What's the EDA Factor?" Ed asked.

"I thought you'd never ask," Charlie chuckled. "It stands for "**Eliminate, Delegate, Automate**.""

Charlie waited for that to sink in and then said, "So, we are going to map the sales cycle, map the sales process for each element of the cycle and then see what we can eliminate, delegate or automate. Sales Kaizen. Pretty neat, huh?"

"We'll see," Ed said. He had been in sales a long time. His skepticism was based on experience; Charlie's enthusiasm was based on theory and speculation.

Charlie sensed the skepticism. "Remember the conversation about leads that we had? Your problem was that the leads were old and cold before you got to them. The idea we came up with…"

"*YOU* came up with," Ed corrected.

"The idea was to have marketing use a series of emails – e-touches they're called – to keep the prospect informed. Or, to use your term, to keep them warm. The system was automated by marketing. In other words, we knew we had to do something so eliminating was not an option. We delegated it to marketing, right? And we showed them how to automate it."

> 00:00
> Every encounter with a customer (phone call, email, invoice, the way your phone is answered) is a "customer touch" and is a part of sales

Charlie held up his coffee mug and said, "Brilliant, if I say so myself."

"Tomorrow we will have our Kaizen team together. How do you want to run it?" Charlie asked.

"You're the Kaizen expert here, what do you think we should do?" Ed answered.

"I gave it some thought. Why don't I give a brief overview of what Kaizen is, how it works, and so forth, and then explain what our outcomes need to be. Since Kaizen for sales is apparently different from other Kaizen events, they will only need an overview."

Charlie continued, "I downloaded some templates from the sales Kaizen web site I was telling you about. We will begin with those and I think we'll be off to a good start. We need to get the room set up and we need to print off some of these sheets. Ready?"

The two men worked all day setting up the room, including a projector so that their findings could be in front of everyone as they were revealed. A couple of flip charts were brought in, the other materials prepared and the two men were ready.

Mike Anderson, the CSO stepped into the conference room just as the men were finishing. "Looks good," Mike said. I like the EDA poster on the wall – that will help keep people focused."

00:00
The CSO is responsible for knowing all aspects of sales strategy, development and management

"You know about EDA?" Ed asked.

"I attended a CSO symposium and one of the topics was Kaizen for Sales. They explained how the EDA process was essential to reducing cycle time in sales. Now I have a question for you two."

The men stopped what they were doing and faced Mike. "How will you know this event was successful?"

Charlie immediately walked over to one of the flip charts, picked up a marker, removed the cap but wrote nothing.

After a brief silence Ed offered, "We will have found ways to shorten the sales cycle."

"That's important," Mike said so Charlie wrote on the flip chart, "Shorten sales cycle".

"What else" Mike asked.

"Okay," Ed said, "we will also need to find a way to help the salespeople make better calls and at a lower cost. We will need to automate as much of the sales process as possible and..."

"Hold on!" Charlie shouted, "I can't write that fast."

After a few minutes of discussion, the three men had developed a list of eight specific outcomes they would need to achieve to feel like the event had been successful.

"Those need to be on the wall right beside the EDA poster," Mike said. "People need to be focused in these events. Now, can you quantify any of those objectives?"

"Like what?" Ed asked.

"Oh, yeah," Charlie interjected. "Like how much faster, how many dollars – things like that."

Mike spoke up, "Yes, exactly. Don't do it now, but when the session opens tomorrow, ask the team to begin thinking about that."

Tuesday would be an interesting day and a new beginning for IVC sales.

CHAPTER TEN: THE EVENT 2

By eight thirty on Tuesday morning the sales Kaizen team had assembled in the conference room and were eagerly enjoying the pastries, juice and coffee. Once seated, the team members introduced themselves to each other and Charlie stood up.

"This is new to all of us. You know sales, I don't. I know Kaizen, you don't. Together, we are going to see how we can refine the sales process at IVC to make it better, faster and, at the same time, reduce the overall cost of sales." As he spoke, Charlie wrote on the flip chart:

Better
Faster
Lower COS

Then he peeled off the page and hung it on the wall in the front of the room.

"We're going to use a process that will become very familiar to you called 'EDA'," and he gestured towards the EDA poster. "The outcomes we want to achieve are over here," and he pointed to the list that had been created the day before. "At any time, if you want to add something to this list, bring it up. It is important that, as soon as possible, we quantify each one of these. We need to be able to measure whether or not we are having the impact we need to have."

Charlie looked at the group. "This may be new and unfamiliar to you right now but, trust me, soon it will all be second nature. I've been through many Kaizen events. Sometimes they get pretty tense, tempers flare and fatigue sets in. That may happen here. Just remember, we are about to do whatever is necessary to make our sales efforts more effective and competitive.

"Let's go over our list." Charlie walked over to the wall where the list was hanging. "Here is what we have so far," and he pointed to the chart which read:

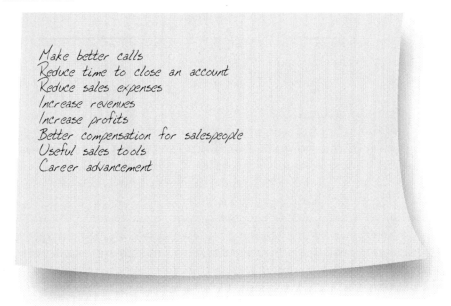

Make better calls
Reduce time to close an account
Reduce sales expenses
Increase revenues
Increase profits
Better compensation for salespeople
Useful sales tools
Career advancement

For the next hour the team discussed the outcomes. Some were refined, some were given varying levels of quantification and everyone had a better understanding of what was expected from the event.

It was time for a break.

Fifteen minutes later, the team was back in the conference room. At each place there was a printed list of the objectives including the revisions that had been added that morning prior to the break. On the screen in front of the room an image was being projected that had the IVC logo, the date, a running digital clock and a series of buttons like those found on web sites. The artwork on the screen matched the artwork on the printed pages that were now in front of each participant. Things were moving fast.

One button on the image on the screen was labeled, "Outcomes".

Charlie stood in front of the group and, using the remote control in his hand, moved the cursor on the screen to the "Outcomes" button and clicked.

"You have this in front of you now. And, again, anytime you feel like we need to make revisions, speak up." He paused for a moment and then asked, "Based on what has happened so far, what have you learned?"

Some of the participants wondered how the changes had been incorporated in the materials as quickly as they had. But none brought it up.

One person said they had never been exposed to Kaizen before and were no longer intimidated by the term. Another said that they were not sure any of this would be worthwhile – they would rather be out selling.

Finally, one person spoke up and asked, "How did you get these color sheets in front of us and the PowerPoint slide updated so quickly?

Charlie smiled and said, "That's the point I was trying to make. With the right attitude and the smart use of technology, we can make better things happen quickly. How many times have we been in meetings where the meeting notes were, well, boring? How many times have we seen presentations that were not up to date?"

Ed took the floor and said, "Now we begin. The first thing we will do is to map our sales cycle. From beginning to end, we want to map out all of the steps that are necessary to close a sale."

As he spoke, Charlie sat down at a laptop and used a mouse to move the cursor on the screen. He clicked on a button labeled, "Cycle" and new screen appeared. At the top were the words, "Sales Cycle". Just below that was a stack of electronic post-it notes. Charlie dragged one down to the center-left of the screen and clicked on it.

Ed asked the group, "What is the first step in the sales cycle, what is the fist thing that we do to close a new account?"

One of the salespeople said, "Well, what works for me is I call the customer, set an appointment and then go out and do a needs analysis. That's what they taught us in sales school and that's what I do. I go out and ask the customer what products they are using now and then I know which one of our products to recommend."

As he spoke, Charlie and Ed exchanged glances and grinned. This was the same thing Ed had said when Charlie first asked him.

Charlie typed in the first post-it note: "Call customer for appointment". Then he dragged another post-it note down, placed it just to the right of the first one and typed in, "Ask about products".

The salesperson who had given the information leaned back in his chair, folded his arms, stared at the screen and nodded agreeing.

"How did you know who to call?" Ed asked.

"It was a lead from the system," the salesperson answered.

Charlie dragged in another post-it note, typed in "Lead" and then placed the note on the same time line as the other two. He had to move the original two notes to the right to make room for the new one.

"How many leads do you typically have at any given time?" Ed was asking the questions with genuine curiosity.

"Well, if we exhibited at a trade show recently there could be hundreds."

"So how do you pick one?"

"Oh, something will stand out. Maybe it's a client I already know or an industry I know something about. Maybe it looks like high potential. There's no real process – I just know it when I see it."

By then, Charlie had added another post-it note to the timeline right after "Leads", one that read "Select". Then he added another post-it note above that one that read "Develop Selection Criteria".

"What if you see more than one account that looks good to you – how do you call that shot?" Ed was asking the questions, everyone was involved in the thinking process, and the salesperson who was giving the information was now leaning forward.

"I use account potential – the bigger sales potential gets the first touch."

Ed asked, "What about urgency? What if a smaller account is ready to buy? If we ignore them to chase the larger accounts, we might lose that sale, right?"

"Well, yeah, but how can I know who is ready to buy and who is not? I have to talk to the customer to figure that out so I might as well talk to the whales rather than the minnows."

"Where do leads come from?" Ed seemed to be changing the subject.

"Marketing."

"What if marketing could provide us with more details, like sense of urgency. Would that help?"

"Sure."

"Okay, now let's see if we can determine what else we would like marketing to give us when they pass a lead to us." Ed was standing by the flip chart ready to record the ideas.

By lunch time the first day, the Kaizen team had determined what criteria marketing would be given. Charlie had also given his ideas for using technology to keeps the leads warm. The team member from the marketing department agreed to go back to her group and see what could be done to give the salespeople better, faster and warmer leads. Everyone agreed that this would make sales happen better and most likely faster.

A long discussion on what criteria needed to be used in prioritizing the accounts had not been as fruitful. Everyone seemed to have their own ideas and all seemed to be valid and valuable.

Some said that the size of the account should be the determining factor. Another said that proximity – being close by – was a distinct advantage because travel would not be needed and would make the local sales faster and lower cost. Someone else suggested that there are industries and applications where the IVC advantage is more obvious, easier to explain and easier to quantify; therefore, that should create a higher priority. All agreed that "gut feel", intuitive knowledge needed to be allowed as well.

At one point, Charlie had clicked on a button on the screen labeled "Help". It took him to the Kaizen for Sales web site. There he found a button labeled "Tools" which he clicked followed by a click on a button labeled "Calculators". Scanning his options, he then clicked on a button labeled "Probability of Sale".

On the screen there was a calculator that would actually compute probability of sale. All eyes in the room were fixed on it. A quick read of the instructions and the intuitive design made using the tool fairly easy.

Five random potential accounts were listed. Then, three main selection criteria were entered followed by what sub-criteria would be used to make the decision. For instance, one criteria was "Revenue Potential" and the sub-criteria for high priority was "High" and the sub-criteria for low priority was "Low".

The team played with the calculator for a while and determined what worked and did not work for the IVC situation. They developed their own criteria and then decided to have their own calculator built, one that would address their specific requirements.

It was lunch time.

The afternoon session was, at once, interesting, tense, productive and frustrating.

When the Kaizen team members returned from lunch, there was a large piece of paper waiting for each of them. This 11 x 17 inch paper had the complete work of the morning on it. In the upper right-hand corner were the objectives. The post-it notes were shown on a horizontal time line.

Interestingly, the original post-it notes, "Call customer for appointment" and "Ask about products" were now steps seven and eight instead of steps one and two as they had been in the beginning of the process. Progress was being made in mapping the sales cycle. Steps that had been overlooked, taken for granted or done casually, were now on the chart.

Only a couple of steps had been identified that could be eliminated. Using tools like the Probability of Sale Calculator were helping with the automation concept. Except for qualifying and quantifying leads, no other steps were found that could be delegated. Whenever the idea of having someone else – or some other department – take on a task, it either proved to be too cumbersome or too expensive. There were few valid opportunities for salespeople to delegate, or so it seemed.

The day ended at five forty-five with the entire sales cycle being mapped. The last step in the cycle was "Referrals". When customers are happy, they will give us referrals. New customers are likely to give us referrals for two reasons: they are happy and, they want someone else to buy what they just bought to validate their buying decision.

> 00:00
> **New customers are more likely to give us referrals than older ones – especially in the case of a competitive win**

Once a salesperson has a referral in hand, they have a lead and that takes them right back to the beginning of the sales cycle.

Some of the Kaizen team decided to go out for a drink. Ed was tired and decided to go home. He called Katherine as he pulled out of the parking lot and each gave the other a brief overview of their day.

Ed was about to hang up when Katherine said, "Ed, would you mind stopping at the store on the way home and pick up some Diet Cokes?"

"Got it," Ed said. "Need anything else?

A few minutes later, Ed was easing his car into a parking place at the Kroger grocery store. He was still preoccupied with the concept of delegating sales tasks when he walked inside Ed made his way to the soft drink aisle and encountered a delivery person from the Coca-Cola Company stocking the shelves with Coke products. Ed picked up a case of Diet Coke from the deliveryman's cart and walked up to the checkout area. He quickly made his way over to the self-checkout area, scanned his drinks, paid for his purchase and walked out to the parking lot.

Then it hit him.

"Whoa!" Ed said out loud as he stopped and stood in the middle of the parking lot. "That's it!"

CHAPTER ELEVEN: DELEGATING

As the sales Kaizen team assembled in the conference room, Ed was pacing excitedly in the front of the room. It was not a nervous pacing but more like anticipation. Ed had an idea that he wanted to present to the group and was anxious to get started.

The new documents that were placed in front of each person's chair included an updated timeline. On this line, every element of the sales cycle that the team had identified the day before was listed. As each person sat down, they looked at the timeline. Some were thinking about how to improve it, some were merely reviewing it and some were thinking about other things – like why they were there instead of back doing their regular job.

Ed began the meeting even before everyone was seated. "I had an ah-ha moment yesterday. A huge ah-ha moment." He walked over to his chair and picked up a case of Diet Coke.

00:00
An "Ah-Ha Moment" is what Tom Peters referred to as a blinding flash of the obvious

"On the way home yesterday my wife asked me to go by the store and pick up some Diet Coke. In other words, I needed to be a buyer because I needed – well, wanted actually – to buy something. I went into the store and found the guy from Coke stocking the shelves. So I picked up a case of Coke from his cart rather than take one he had just put on the shelf. I walked up to the front and found the self-checkout line, scanned the product, paid and was out in the parking lot in no time at all. That's when it hit me."

Ed put down the case of Diet Coke, folded his arms and said, "What did the people at Kroger do in this transaction?" He waited a moment and then said, "Nothing!"

He unfolded his arms, walked towards one of the flip charts, picked up a marker and said, "Kroger has the vendor supplying the product and making it available for purchase. The consumer manages the entire transaction – get it?"

Ed let that sink in and then said, "Kroger delegates the sales process to the customer! We can do the same thing. Yesterday we were stuck trying to figure out who the salesperson could delegate to. Why not delegate to the customer?"

Ed wrote across the top of the flip chart: Customer Managed Transactions. "Let's brainstorm this for just a moment and see what we have."

With that, Ed drew a vertical line down the center of the paper, making two columns. He placed a "+" sign at the top of the left column and a "-" sign at the top of the right column.

"First, let's talk about the positive aspects of this. What are the advantages of having the customer manage most of the sales process?"

Ed wrote down the ideas as they were thrown out. In a few minutes the chart looked like this:

The discussion then centered around how each of the negatives could be neutralized. It was decided that routine sales like restocking orders could be automated and then delegated to the customers. A system would be put in place to notify the appropriate sales person whenever a customer managed a sale just in case there was need for the salesperson to follow up.

"What else could we delegate to our customers?" Ed asked. "What customer activities are taking up a lot of time for us that the customer could do independently?"

"Product demos take more time than anything else," one of the team members responded. "But there's no way the customer can do a product demo."

"Okay, let's look at that through the Kaizen lens, or process, for a moment." Ed walked over to the other flip chart. "What are the steps involved in a product demo?"

Customer Managed Relations

+	−
Low cost	No personal touch
No labor cost for us	What happens to relationship?
Little time investment for us	Customer may not be making the best decision:
Saves the customer time	• What if we have a new product?
Customer can buy anytime – even when we are not available	• New program? • New pricing?
Frees up salespeople for other sales	Competition could do the same thing; we become a commodity
	Do we want to do internet sales?

"Well, it varies by product or service, of course. Essentially, we take one of our units out, set it up and show the customer how it works."

Ed thought for a minute and asked, **"Is the customer more interested in how it works or what it will do for them?"**

"Again, it depends on the customer contact. The executives want to now what it will do for them but the technical folks want to see the flashing lights, the data output, the connection panels, things like that."

"So, are you saying that the decision makers want to know what it will do and the decision influencers want to know how it does it?"

"Well, yes, I suppose you could say it that way."

00:00 Customers want to know specifically what our product or service will do for them right now

"Good," Ed continued, "we could close the sale with the decision maker without even showing the device if we had done a comprehensive needs analysis earlier, right?"

"Sometimes."

"In those situations, would the technical folks want interaction with the box or would observation of the box be enough?"

"I'm not following you."

"Here's what I'm thinking. What if we had something on our web site that would answer all or most of the technical person's issues? They could go to the site, see various views of the box in various stages, they could download comprehensive spec sheets and they could find contact information for talking to some of our techs."

Ed was interrupted by another member of the team. "Better yet, we could make it sort of like a video game. How hard could that be? For instance, the tech would click on a picture of the device they wanted to evaluate, then they could show inputs or scenarios that their organization would be likely to encounter and then they would se how our devices react."

00:00 How many routine sales tasks could be managed by your customers on your web site?

Another member of the team interjected, "Yeah, I used a site like that when I was setting up my home theater. I clicked on the connectors that were shown on the image and as I did, a pop-up told me what the impedance would be for each connection and which components would be best for each. It is being done already."

"Would creating that level of interaction and animation be expensive?" Ed asked.

"I don't know, but I doubt it. There are high school and even middle school kids in my neighborhood developing their own computer games so it can't be impossible. And aren't there web sites where you can find programmers?"

00:00 Look for parallel ideas from other industries

Another team member interjected, "A friend of mine used, what was it, oh, yeah, Elance.com. He had programmers all over the world bidding on his project. Had it done quickly and, as I recall, pretty inexpensively."

Ed was making notes on the flip chart.

After a while, the sales Kaizen team appointed two people to look at the alternatives for providing product demos online and to make a recommendation back to the team.

A break was called but few people left the room. They were engaged in animated conversations about how the product demo scenario, if it worked out, would give the salespeople significantly more selling time. Some talked about their experiences with similar technologies on other web sites.

When the session reconvened, Ed began talking about another step in the sales process but Charlie interrupted him.

"Before we move on to that, Ed, we need to complete one more step from the previous exercise. We need to quantify, as well as possible, what the impact of that might be. What percentage of the typical salesperson's time is spent doing product demos for the customer's technical people?"

"Probably twenty percent," said one member of the team.

"If everything goes well, maybe!" interjected another member. "In the real world, it is not uncommon for the technical person to ask the rep a question they cannot answer. The rep has to contact one of our technical folks, get the answer and go back to the customer. I think it's more like thirty percent."

After some discussion, the team decided to split the difference and say twenty-five percent of the salesperson's time would be spent on product demos. So Charlie asked the next question, "What will the salespeople do with this time and what will that be worth to the company?"

"Oh," joked one member of the team, "about a hundred million dollars!"

"You may be close," Charlie said surprisingly. "What were our revenues last year?"

A team member suggested, "We broke the four hundred million dollar mark for the first time in November, right?"

If we gave our salespeople twenty-five percent more selling time then, theoretically, they could generate twenty-five percent more revenue. That's one hundred million dollars."

There was a noticeable silence in the room.

"But let's say that giving the salespeople twenty-five percent more selling time allows them to do other things in addition to selling and let's also assume that all demos could not be replaced. Let's say the net result is only a five percent increase in sales. How much is that?"

Ed wrote on the flipchart: <u>$2,000,000!!</u>

As he wrote, Ed exclaimed, "We just came up with a two-million dollar idea!"

Charlie laughed and said, "Ed, it's true what you say. You salespeople don't do numbers. I think you're missing a zero."

"What!?!" Ed made some calculations in the margin of the flipchart and said, "Oh, my gosh. You're right. This is a twenty-million dollar idea!"

The idea now took on greater importance.

Over the course of the next two days, the team worked through several more steps in the sales cycle and the related processes for each step. In all, they estimated they had reduced the selling time by just over forty percent and had found six million dollars in cost reductions and a potential seventy-seven million dollars in revenue enhancements.

What the group could not assess was how much better the sales activities would be going forward. Their mandate had been "better, faster, lower COS" and assessing "better" had proven to be difficult. With the significant accomplishments of this Kaizen event, however, the team felt like having another event to primarily address the issue of "better" would be a worthwhile endeavor.

The final document that came from this event was a virtual how-to book for sales at IVC. It was so comprehensive that if IVC had decided to use distributors, value-added resellers (VAR's) or any other distribution channel, this document would show the indirect reps how to sell the IVC line. There was no plan to use anyone other than the direct sales force, but the document made assessing the feasibility of using an indirect sales channel relatively straightforward.

No one on the team could anticipate the impact this event would have on IVC or how quickly the results would be felt.

CHAPTER TWELVE: GAME OVER

Three months later the sales activities at IVC bore little resemblance to the way they were conducted ninety days earlier. At least for most salespeople.

Two subsequent sales Kaizen events had been conducted. One had focused on making better sales calls and the other focused on compensation.

The second Kaizen event opened with a discussion about what the word "better' meant. If the sales calls were going to be better, what did that mean?

Some of the flip charts that eventually made their way to the final documents were:

What is "Better"?

Lower cost

Less time in front of customer

Less time planning call

Less non-productive time

- Travel

- Answering follow-up questions

More effective communication

- Visuals

- Collateral materials

Solution-based, not product or feature based

Qualified and quantified value to the customer

Lower costs

Replace face-to-face calls whenever practical

- Video emails

- Web-based tools

- Interactive PowerPoint and PDF documents

Less travel

- Better territory management

- Realign territories

Geographic vs. "Vertical" account assignments

Less time

Automate / delegate pre-call planning

- Client profile pre-populated by marketing

- Use online data bases

Faster written responses

- Template RFP responses

- Easy access to collateral materials for forwarding

- Boilerplate paragraphs, charts, graphs

Faster PowerPoint presentations

- Templates by application

- Easily customizable

Pre-Call submission - send detailed info to customer the day before the call

Solution based sales

Templates based on specific problems

Library of customer problems

- How to detect

- How to quantify

- What solutions we offer

- Benefits to customer

Case studies, war stories and testimonials

Walking through the Atlanta sales office ninety days after the initial sales Kaizen was a different experience. There was electricity in the air, a sense that a lot was going on even though there seemed to be a lack of hustle and bustle.

Most salespeople were sitting in their cubicles wearing headsets with microphones. A casual observer might think this was a basic call center. It was, however, the next generation of sophisticated sales operations.

All one had to do was to listen in on any of the conversations and they would realize this was no ordinary sales environment.

In one cubicle, a senior sales rep, Sarah, was talking directly at her laptop while holding up one of IVC's newest devices. "As you can see, Mr. Yancey," she was saying, "our new frequency regeneration unit is significantly smaller and, as you might suspect, consumes significantly less power. What I am holding here is actually a module with four regenerators that.., I'm sorry? Yes, that's right four units. Small, huh? They fit right in to your 1760 racks and no rewiring is necessary. What? Right. Four units now fit in less space as one. Does this mean you can continue your growth rate without adding shelves?"

Sarah clicked her mouse and continued, "On the bottom left of your screen is a button labeled "Specifications". If you click on that you will have a copy of all of the specs on this device. Matt Parker in your IT department expressed some concerns about our FDM protocol and all of his concerns are addressed in this document. You can forward this to him or I can send him a copy – which would be easier for you?"

> 00:00
> Sales automation tools make closing larger sales easier and easier – but never easy

She waited for the answer, "Fine, thanks, I sent it. It should be in his inbox about right now. And if you will click on the button labeled "Benefits" you will see a summary of what we have been discussing, including a cost justification that shows that your IRR payback will be an incredible three months based on Phase One which, you said, would be 1135 units right?"

Sarah paused as she listened to the customer. "Yes, that's right. If you scroll down on the cost justification tool, you will see that all calculations were based on the 1135 units to be included in Phase One. What were you thinking?"

After another pause, she continued, "We are hearing that a lot; everyone's power costs seem to be going up. Maybe it's the price of oil. We used .045 as the computation factor for KWH, what is it now?"

> **00:00**
> Customers appreciate interactive tools that allow them to conduct their own analysis

Another pause, "That's actually a pretty good rate from what I am hearing. We can recalculate your savings, if you like. I can do it or you can simply place your cursor in the KWH box and enter the new rate. Try it. Cool, huh?"

Patiently, Sarah listened for nearly three minutes and then said, "You know, that might be the best for you guys. If we implement Phases One and Two at the same time, your savings will increase in more locations immediately. When you consider you will have smaller units consuming less power, generating less heat and, best of all, giving you and your customers a 33% boost in output, the more units you can install now the more your revenue will go up and your expenses go down. Do you want me to process the paperwork now for both Phases?"

While she was waiting for a response and email popped into her inbox. It was from Matt Parker in the customer's IT department. She continued her call with the customer, "Of course, you will need Matt's check-off on the protocol. Wait, I just got an email from him – let me see what it says. You too, okay, let's see what he is saying."

She opened the email which was a copy of an email Matt had sent to her customer contact, Yancey. "Looks like he's satisfied. We have enough units in stock to begin the installs the day after tomorrow. We will work from the implementation table in our agreement. However, if at any time you want to change the order of the installations, you can do it online. You can always call me, of course, but if you want to save time, we have a place on the web where you or anyone you designate can manage the implementation. I just sent you an email with the IP address and the initial password. Change the password to whatever you like."

> **00:00**
> Celebrate your wins!

Sarah quietly raised her hands in the air with a "Rocky" victory gesture. Her voice on the telephone remained professional.

"Thank you, Mr. Yancey, this…"

"Okay, John, thank you, *John.* This is going to set you guys another step ahead of your competitors. Well done!"

As soon as the call was over, she called her manager, Rick Harper, to celebrate the sale. Mike Anderson, the CSO was in Rick's office at the time. As soon as Rick heard the energy in her voice, he put her call on the speakerphone. "Mike's in here – do you want him to hear what you have to say?"

"You bet," she said. "Yancey just placed his order – do I have the first sale of the new FDM's?"

Laughing, Rick answered, "You sure do – what will you do with the bonus money?"

"Haven't thought about it – and I haven't told you the best part yet."

"Okay, we're waiting. We're two very busy and very important people, you know," Mike said kidding.

"They're going with Phase One and Phase Two!"

There was a long silence. Finally Rick asked, "How many units?"

"1135 in Phase One, 4410 in Phase Two". It was all she could do not to scream out the numbers.

"Okay, I'm doing the math here – that looks like a, let's see, whoa! That's a $1.4 million sale."

"Something's wrong with your math, Rick. I show $1.62 million and some change."

"Did you forget the price break at 5000 units?" Rick asked.

"Didn't forget it and didn't offer it. The quantity discount wasn't needed. Look, his IRR will be here before Labor Day and his ROI, which I did not even have to mention by the way, is not much longer. And if they are hit with another power rate increase at any of their facilities, the payback 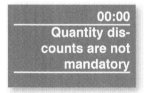 will only get better. Plus, he is saving his biggest account; GE was about to go with a competitor because of the throughput issue…"

"Stop selling, Sarah!" Rick yelled. "We get it."

Sarah added, "Besides, giving the additional discount would not bring me as closer to my Mini!"

Sarah had a miniature Cooper Mini car on her desk right in front of her poster with pictures of her other goals: the downtown condo, the Greek Isle cruise, and others. She opened and closed the doors on her miniature car as she spoke.

> **00:00**
> **Successful people visualize their success long before it is a reality**

Mike spoke into the speaker phone as he asked, "How long have you been working on this sale?

"Let's see. Eight weeks ago they threw us out because they were standardizing on someone else's protocol because of the throughput issue. An engineer and I went out there and muddied the water long enough to conduct a Q/Q [Qualified and Quantified] needs analysis. We found all kinds of stuff, sent a proposal as an interactive PDF, followed up with a few e-touches and than made one more face-to-face. We had to scramble, and we got it."

> **00:00**
> **Even "lost" sales can be won back by sophisticated salespeople**

In another cubicle a sales rep seemed to be chanting incoherently. He was saying, "John. Mr. Rockland. Mary. Sam," and a host of other names. He was clicking his mouse between each name.

> **00:00**
> **Real Sales Automation can cause strange habits and bring great results**

What he was actually doing is recording a voice greeting for some new contacts who would receive his video blog the next day. The personal touch paid handsome dividends.

All throughout the office, the salespeople who were there were doing similar tasks. The ones who were not there were doing the same things from their home offices or on the road.

One of the most interesting indicators of how things were changing was the daily sales report. On this day, Sarah was number five on the list but with the Yancey sale, that would change and put her on the top of the list.

Bubba was continuing to have one of his best years ever. His sales were up over the previous year, yet, he was now second from the bottom on the list. His peers were easily passing him by because Bubba had decided that the new way of selling was not necessary. "The only cost justification I need is a couple of tickets to a Falcons game!" he would say.

Interestingly, Bubba was already out of the sales game and he did not even know it. He would be leaving IVC in the next few weeks, but he did not know it yet. He would not be fired; it would be his reluctant choice.

> **00:00**
> Some people are out of the game before they realize it. Not adapting to change is the most common reason

The sales Kaizen event that focused on compensation resulted in a major change in the way salespeople were paid. A quick look at a page from the flip chart explained it all:

Compensation

Goal: ~~revenue market share unit sales industry leader innovator~~ profit!

Extra compensation:

1) Product pushes

2) Target markets, industries

3) Manager-directed

Change every six months

Compensation for the salespeople would now be calculated on profit, not revenue. The discussion in the session had gone back and forth until one member of the team reminded everyone that the company ran on profits, new products were developed through profits, executives and some managers were compensated on profits and investors were expecting profits.

Bubba was an old-school salesperson. Most of his sales were made based on price reductions and, often, significant price reductions. The margins on most of his sales were so low that he stood to take a major cut in his income when the compensation program became profit-based. Another factor was that he would also be held accountable for his COS and those football tickets would now count against his income.

For the traditional salesperson, the writing was on the wall – or at least on the flipchart. The old game was over.

EPILOGUE: NEW GAME

It is being played in all industries and in all parts of the world. Business-to-Business salespeople as well as Business-to-Consumer salespeople are capitalizing on the advantages that come from sales sophistication. As sales professional, sales leader or Chief Sales Officer, you have the option of embracing, ignoring or resisting the changes that are happening in sales. Whatever you decide, your customers will be just fine. If your organization does not embrace them, one of your competitors will and your customers can begin doing business with them.

Sales is a measurable, predictable and replicatable science.

More and more of the sales processes are being automated. Customers are changing the way they want to interact with vendors and the alert providers are addressing those changes.

Customers are expecting a more qualified and quantified answer to the question, "Why should I pay more for your product/service?"

Discounting is a dangerous, addictive process. The more the salesperson uses it, the more they want or need to use it. It eventually leads to a sale with no profit and companies run on profit.

Now, what will you do differently?

"In the history of recorded time no customer has ever said, 'Your price is too high,' and meant it."

-Chuckism #6

WANT MORE?

Use this book as a sales coaching tool.

I am a big believer in Do-It-Yourself sales coaching. There are a couple of ways you can use this book with your sales team. One is to have everyone read it and then review it in a single session. The other way is to break up the review sessions into several smaller ones. Either way, there are some tools you can use – they're free - just download them from the web sites:

To learn how to implement all of the ideas in this book – and much more about professional selling, go to:

www.SaleSSuiteS.com

www.NANOSECONDSALESPERSON.com

There you will find tools like:

- Leader's guide
- Student handout materials
- Access to sales tools similar to the ones mentioned in the story

If you would like more information on Kaizen for Sales simply go to:

www.KAIZENFORSALES.com

ABOUT THE AUTHOR

Chuck Reaves, CSP, CPAE, CSO is a professional speaker, trainer and consultant specializing in advanced value-added selling. A former top salesperson for AT&T, he was the highest producer among 1,100 sales professionals.

His first book, The Theory of 21 has been translated into Japanese and widely circulated throughout Japan.

Chuck has helped large and mid-market companies increase their profits by teaching their sales teams how to raise their prices and their volumes simultaneously. He speaks about 100 times each year to audiences all around the world. He has made more than 650 presentations to TEC/Vistage groups internationally and is one of their highest rated speakers on the subject of sales.

For his volunteer work, Chuck has been named Veteran's Advocate of the year, and Outstanding Georgia Citizen and has received recognition from two US Presidents and other dignitaries. Of the four thousand members of the National Speakers Association, Chuck is one of only 150 to have received the Certified Speaking Professional (CSP) and Speakers Hall of Fame (CPAE) designations. He is a decorated Vietnam veteran and a successful entrepreneur.

He has been introduced as "The Peter Drucker of Sales" and as "The CSO Guru".

CONTACT INFORMATION

How can Chuck Reaves help you?

    Help you help your salespeople?

        Help you help your customers help their customers?

Chuck provides speaking, training, consulting, coaching and sales technology assistance. To inquire about his availability, contact your preferred speakers bureau or contact him directly at:

Chuck@ChuckReaves.com

1.800 MR. REAVES (800.677.3283)
770.965.5595

5952 Allee Way
Braselton, GA 30517

CHUCKISMS

SUCCESS

1. For every person who will say yes, there are twenty who will say no; for a positive response you must find the twenty-first person. – The Theory of 21

2. The only difference in you and the person who is doing what you would like to do is just that: they're doing it.

3. There are no extraordinary people; there are only ordinary people who are doing things that others perceive to be extraordinary.

SALES

4. There are two types of people in the world: those who know they are in sales and those who don't.

5. No one is ever going to pay you what your product or service is worth. They will pay you more than that or they will pay you less than that based on what they think it's worth, and we control their thinking.

6. In the history of recorded time, no customer has ever said, "Your price is too high", and meant it.

7. If the person I'm talking to cannot understand the difference in cost and price I am selling to the wrong person.

8. To satisfy a desire, people will pay *MORE*; to satisfy a need, people will pay *QUICKLY*.

9. The person at the table who knows the most about the other person's business wins.

10. If I want the accolades for the win, I must take accountability for the loss.

Customer Servic*ing*

11. Your customers will no longer compare your level of customer service with that of your competitor; they will now compare your level of service with that of every vendor they deal with – personally and professionally.

Management

12. My people will live up to or down to my expectations.

13. My people are more likely to follow my tracks than the sound of my voice.

14. Tie your compensation to your expectations – a rule that every company violates.

Sales Management

15. The questions you ask your salespeople will determine what they say and do when they're in front of their customers.

Leadership

16. If you look back over your shoulder and no one is following you, you are not a leader.

Goals

17. A goal is not a goal unless it is written, quantified and dated.

18. All a goal does is to help us recognize inevitable opportunities.

Change

19. There are two ways to respond to change: capitalize on it or capsize under it.

20. Change is inevitable, change brings opportunity; therefore, change is an inevitable opportunity.

Made in the USA
Charleston, SC
01 February 2012